Art Media Series

Creating with Puppets

Lothar Kampmann

 Van Nostrand Reinhold Company/New York

Illustrations
Illustrations in the technical section are from the author; the students of the Ruhr Training College for Elementary Teachers, Dortmund section; the Puppet Theatre Collection of Munich (pp. 3, 4, 13,); Puppet Theatre Society; "Die Spielbude" of Nürnberg (pp. 35, 43); David Strasmann and Co., Wuppertal-Ronsdorf. Illustrations in the Appendix: Kindergarten work, students' work, Puppet Theatre Society "Die Spielbude" under the direction of Reiner Schlamp, Hans-Sachs Gymnasium, Nürnberg; Puppet Theatre Collection of Munich (pp. 66—74).
Photographs by Wilhelm Hohmann, Recklinghausen; Munich Puppet Theatre Collection; Reiner Schlamp, Nürnberg; Werner Stuhler-Bavaria (p. 43).

Sponsored by the Günther Wagner Pelikan-Werke, Hanover; and Koh-I-Nor, Inc., 100 North Street, Bergen, New Jersey 08804.

Published in the United States of America, 1972, by Van Nostrand Reinhold Company, a Division of Litton Educational Publishing, Inc., 450 West 33rd Street, New York, N.Y. 10001.

16 15 14 13 12 11 10 9 8 7 6 5 4 3 2 1

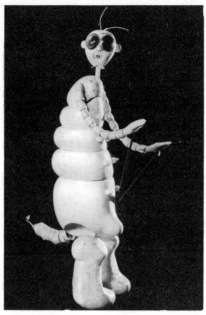

Right: Rod-puppet, 'Ghost'
from 'Nightpiece' by
R. Tescher, Vienna, 1913

Left: Glove puppet of
Jan Klaasen, the Dutch
Punch, with Katrina,
19th century

Foreword

'The Puppet play is blessed by
God, and because of this it will
never die' says an Indian proverb.

Puppetry is indeed an ancient art
and is known by many names and
under many guises in every coun-
try. Puppets have been used from
earliest times to the present day.
They were the dolls which were
buried in the graves of great
Egyptians to represent servants
who would otherwise have been
sacrificed. They were used to
personify the gods in Oriental
Mystery Plays. They became fetish
dolls said to be endowed with the
powers of ancestors and, of course,
the dolls with which we played as
children. But, to most of us,
puppets are figures which, with
rigid features but lively gestures,
speak their lines from a miniature
stage.

George Bernard Shaw once wrote
that the dramatic influence puppets had on him was greater than
that of live actors. He said that
puppets, with their stiff expression
and unnatural posture, give an
impression of old pictures and
glass, and, despite their rigidity,
seem to be more alive than the
spectators who stand and watch
them.

Puppets insinuate themselves and
their opinions into our minds. They
are mere objects of wood and
cloth, mere dolls which obey the
hand that controls them and have
no will of their own. In that lies

3

their charm and their educative influence, for their effect on us is deeper than if they resembled ourselves.

Three aspects of puppetry have educational value: the making, the performance, and the watching and listening. In this book we deal with the making and staging of puppets. There are four basic types of puppets — glove, shadow, rod and string. We shall deal with the simplest and cheapest as well as the complicated, taking care that in every case they really can be made at home or in the classroom.

Many books have been written on the art of manipulating puppets, and there are definite techniques in moving the hands and using the voice. Children tend to do these things automatically and without thinking, just as they accept, more readily than adults, the puppets as actors.

It is just as Goethe said: 'This childish entertainment and activity produced in me such a capability to create and to act, and had exercised and demanded such skill and technique, as perhaps could have occurred in no other way, in so short a time and confined a space.

Javanese shadow-theatre

Home-made Puppets

Dolls were our very first playmates. It never mattered how big or small, or how they were made, we gave them names and a big place in our child's world, for dolls are the interpreters of a child's thoughts and desires. They are friends, never too tired to play, never older or wiser than the child itself. They never take offence and always give the answer wished for, since the child answers its own questions. Little wonder that children give their whole affection to them.

Those were the dolls with which we played; here we deal with puppets which can be 'played' — which assume the role of actor, and at which we look and listen. Punch and Judy are examples.

In this book, as we introduce the various types of puppets and some of the countless styles, we shall move from the simple to the complicated, and suggest ideas for puppets that can be used dramatically.

The gifts of imagination and invention play the biggest part; the material is subordinate. Artists and children display these gifts at their best, differentiated only by the standard of perfection they achieve.

First Improvisation

Any object in a child's world can be a plaything: ordinary, everyday implements such as bottles, slippers, eggwhisks can become puppets. They are taken over unchanged and endowed with personalities. An example of this would be the small child's game of 'Fork is Mother and Spoon is Father' in which a spoon and fork are given features with wax crayons (easily washed off) and hair of bunched wool.

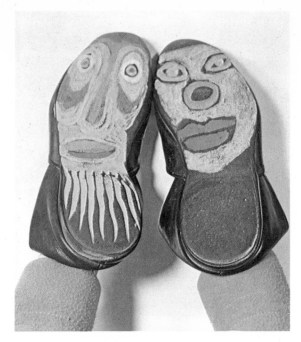

Slippers can be turned into puppets by crayoning features on the soles, and inserting a hand to provide support and animation. They can be made to appear to talk, or to dance together.

Spoon Puppets

We will use wooden spoons to make our first real puppets. Given arms and properly painted and dressed they will have a different character and improved appearance from those decorated with crayon or coloured paper. It is advisable to give the spoons a coat of size before attempting to paint them, as this will seal the pores of

the wood and permit a smoother flow of paint. A wire or wooden cross-piece is attached to form the shoulders and arms, after which they can be dressed, and hands of card or felt glued on. These 'scarecrow' puppets are limited in their expression by their rigid limbs. If they are to appear 'on stage' it is an advantage if the arms can be made to move. To do this tie the arms with thread securely, but flexibly, to the shank of the spoon — a spot of glue will seal the knot.

Rod Puppets

Now we have puppets with moveable arms, but these arms merely dangle and swing when the puppet is turned from side to side. To make them move purposefully, attach thin rods of wire to the wrists with thread, flexibly of course. By adapting the wooden spoon puppet the job is half done, but it is far more satisfying to build a complete puppet from the beginning. A length of $\frac{1}{2}''$ dowel (or broomstick) will serve for the body, with wire or wooden arms

fastened as for the wooden spoon puppet. The most important part is the head which can be made from a wooden ball, or old tennis ball or modelled from a polystyrene block. All these can be painted with poster colour or pasted with coloured paper.

Puppets created with a collage of magazine illustrations are especially lively. Plastic adhesive can be used to fasten on features cut from illustrations like eyes, ears, nose and hair to the wooden

ball, tennis ball or polystyrene block. You can also use buttons for eyes, string for eyebrows and hair, a cork for a nose and cardboard for the ears. It is as well to give the ball a coat of size before painting or pasting. When complete the colours can be made fast with a coating of library paste. *Do not varnish polystyrene* as varnish contains a solvent.

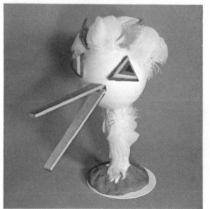

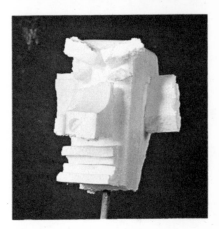

Tin-can puppets can be particularly effective, but with the labels left unpainted classroom project-work is enlivened. Another dimension is added by the sound effects produced when they knock together.

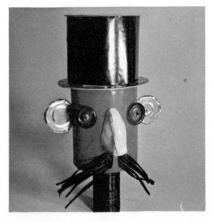 

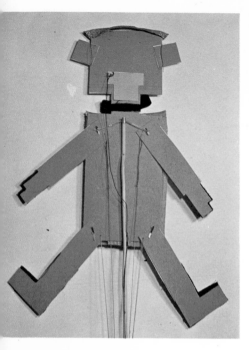

The Jumping Jack puppet belongs to the group of jointed, 'playable' puppets. It is made of cardboard and has very simple movements. The limbs are activated in lever fashion when the ring, to which all the strings are tied, is pulled. The joints can be made with paper fasteners, as the illustration shows. Generally the puppet is hung against a background to prevent spinning, its movements therefore are limited to a single plane when the ring is pulled.

The repertoire of Jumping Jack can be further developed by turning him into a rod puppet and giving the limbs independent movement by pulling their strings individually. The rod must be fastened firmly to the body.

This puppet can be operated from above, like a marionette, providing the strings are fastened to the hands and feet.

Shadow Plays

Now to a type of rod puppet which has a particular purpose. This is the shadow puppet which, despite its long history of use in traditional plays of the Far East, still enjoys a wide popularity. The puppet is held, and operated

against a white sheet and in front of a strong light which illuminates the sheet whilst the black figures act their play in silhouette. The silhouettes need not always be solid black. Paler, and sometimes coloured shadows will add excitement to the play. Solid figures can be made in outline resembling black-on-white drawings. The outlines thus formed can be filled in with coloured transparent paper. A combination of these methods gives the shadow play a charming effect of black outline and glowing colour.

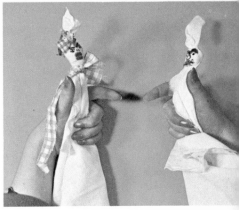

Simple Hand Puppets

The knot puppet is probably the simplest form of hand puppetry and has been traced back to the very beginning of the art. A handkerchief is held in the palm of the hand with a knot tied in it to represent the head. The thumb and middle finger act as arms whilst the index finger supports the head and gives it movement: its appearance is enhanced by the painting of a face and by dressing it up with scraps of other materials. This type of puppet can be given more character by decorating a small cardboard tube with paint or coloured paper and fitting it over the knot. It has now ceased to be just a simple handkerchief.

Puppet Heads

Another simple kind of puppet is the finger puppet created by fitting a cardboard tube over the index finger to form the head and neck.

If the tube you wish to use is too loose, a better fit can be obtained by winding a strip of card around the inside of the tube as shown in the illustration. A circle of thick string is glued around the neck to act as a shoulder support for the clothing.

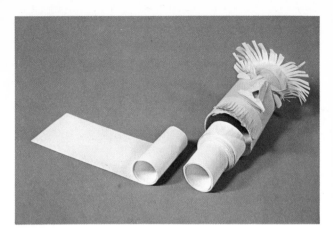

The clothes are simply made: the pattern consists of two identical shapes (front and back, as illustrated) that are stitched together and then turned right-side out to form a glove. A coloured draw-thread can be used to pull the neck together above the ring of string. A number of these dresses can be made easily and cheaply to facilitate the quick changes of costume necessary to the progress of the play.

Very practical puppet heads can be made from corrugated paper which is wound around the finger and drawn down slightly, making a tubelike neck. Take care to leave a small ridge at the base of the neck to act as a shoulder support for the clothing. In trimming and decorating this type of head much can be done to create exciting and dramatic features using pieces of

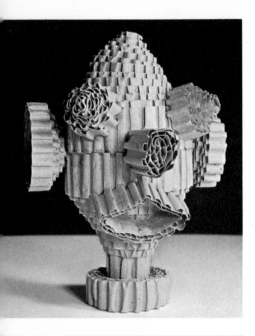

corrugated paper. Before painting, seal the head with library paste, as described on page 10.

The cardboard tube can also be used as a base on which to build a featured head using a plastic modelling material, that moulds like clay and dries hard, which can be obtained from art shops. The tube should first be sealed and then coated with a plastic material so as to provide a key; when this is dry thicker layers can be added for modelling.

You may prefer to use the cheaper paper-layer method. Begin by winding many layers of well-pasted paper around the tube, building up the foundation for the features, which can be formed by using layers of paste-soaked tissue paper that is pinched and squeezed into shape.

Painting the head completes the job. All colouring will be improved by matt varnishing which also makes the head more durable.

Now let us deal with heads modelled in the real sense of the word. The simplest way is to use the plastic modelling material, which dries bone-hard and will stand the knocking-about it will receive in children's play. The head can be painted or varnished.

In these pictures the tube puppet is painted, pasted and dressed according to fancy. It is worked by hand, being grasped at the lower end.

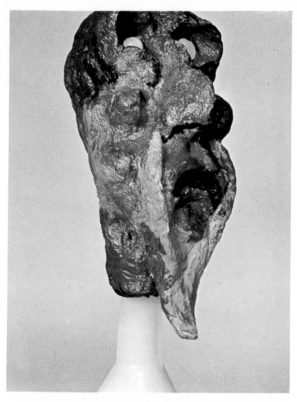

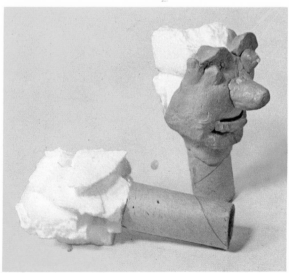

This solid head will possibly be too heavy for your requirements, and in this case, polystyrene can be the answer. This is very light, and the plastic modelling material very hard and durable, even in thin layers. So these two materials are an ideal combination. Make a thin 'pancake' of the modelling material and lay it over the polystyrene block, covering it completely, not forgetting to roll a finger tube and to insert it firmly into the block. In a reasonably short time the plastic modelling material is dry and hard, and then the features, etc. can be added to this base.

Perhaps not so light but cheaper is the papier-mâché head. This can be made in several ways. One

is to roll and crumple newspaper into a firm ball, binding it well with string and gluing a finger tube into it. Now wind paper strips, well coated with paste, tightly around it to give it form and firmness. Paper torn up very fine and kneaded with paste is used to form the details and features, and a matchstick can serve as an inner support for a long nose, for instance. Do not use too much paste as it makes the material soggy and is then difficult to shape. Papier-mâché heads are not easy to hold and work on. So mould them on to a stick which can be stuck into a bottle neck to dry. This takes some time, but when the head is finally painted and matt-varnished it will seem worth the effort.

22

At this stage hands and feet can be added to the glove, the former being fastened to cardboard tubes into which thumb and finger can be inserted so that the arms can gesticulate. When making the hands, especially if they are to have separate fingers, and whether plastic modelling material or papier-mâché is used, it is advisable to make a little framework of wire which can be fastened to the arm tube. For the feet, which only dangle, little wooden blocks, painted and varnished, will suffice.

Mask Puppets

Now for a brief incursion into the realm of the mask puppet. The mask is pulled over the head of the child who then becomes the puppet. For this, too, we need a tube, a cylinder big enough to go over the head, ears and nose, and to rest on the shoulders. One can then determine where the eyes are to be, for the player must see, of course! The illustration shows some of the many ways one can make and decorate such masks.

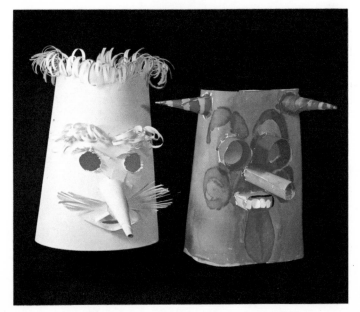

A Variety of Heads

The paper-layer method of construction lends itself readily to the modelling of more realistic features whilst maintaining strength with lightness. The basic model is made from Plasticine, using modelling tools to obtain the fine detail. A coating of paste is applied to the surface of the model on to which is laid layer upon layer of tissue paper each coated with paste. As tissue paper is so thin at least eight layers are necessary. To ensure a proper coverage use a different colour tissue for alternate layers. When the head is *completely* dry cut it down the middle with a sharp knife and remove the Plasticine. The two halves are

glued together and the joint made good with a few layers of pasted tissue. When dry the head can be painted and matt-varnished.

If an even more durable head is required plastic wood, instead of

paper-layers, is applied $\frac{1}{8}''$ thick over the Plasticine after applying a coat of petroleum jelly. When *completely* dry this material can be sanded to a really fine finish.

Puppet heads can be created from a wide variety of materials and from table tennis balls, skittles and tennis balls, etc. But finally we must mention those carved from wood. As these are solid they are comparatively heavy, and though durable, are perhaps best left to the more skilled. The best woods for the purpose are lime, maple and poplar. Balsa wood is very light and easy to cut and finish, but is easily damaged.

Before we move on to the marionettes, a few words on a lively, inexpensive and, in fact, edible form of puppetry: the Vegetable Theatre. Apples, pears, oranges, onions, lettuce, potatoes, carrots, etc., are the actors. Stuck on to a stick, around which is tied a napkin or duster, each fruit or vegetable can play its own role – the sharp onion, the bitter lemon, the playful lettuce and the down-to-earth carrot – even if only to speak of its own qualities. Naturally the life of these actors is ephemeral and they therefore should be returned to the kitchen as soon as possible after the final curtain!

Marionettes

In contrast to the puppets shown so far (glove, finger and rod puppets) marionettes are simply puppets whose movements are controlled, usually from above, solely by strings. The principle is shown here in its clearest and simplest form. A string tied to a piece of cloth and jerked about quickly or slowly causes the cloth to dance and leap about. A bigger

cloth, suspended from a stick by two or more strings is a further step towards the marionette. While one hand moves the stick in the general direction, the other makes particular movements by pulling on the individual strings.

Interesting marionettes can easily be developed with limited materials. Attaching additional strings or, say, little blocks of wood immediately creates a new actor, and the way is open to the abstract marionette.

The tin-can snake can shuffle and prance and rattle about the stage.

The looped and hanging chain suggests ideas for other performers.

The Beer Mat Phantom.

The Spiral Beast.

There is virtually nothing which cannot be employed in the production of this kind of marionette. All these objects have characters of their own and can be given parts to play. A look through the junk in the attic or cellar will often reward you with the unlikely object suitable for this purpose.

The marionettes shown up to now have been abstract characters, simple movement being their primary qualification. They have not reached the stage of having limbs which move independently, and are restricted by their limited capabilities. When one leaves this type for the figure marionette, the possibilities are endless.

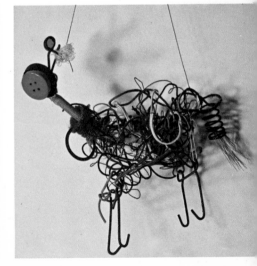

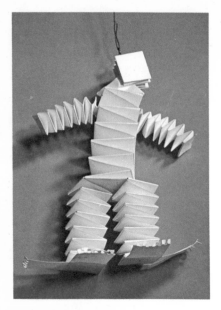

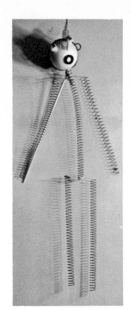

In these puppets the materials are used in their natural state, but are reshaped and reorganized.

Controlling the Figures

When one looks at these new figures it is immediately obvious that the simple string control is not going to be sufficient. The more elaborate the figure, the more intricate and elegant the possibilities of movement. The apparatus controlling the movement has to function accurately, as one motion often depends on another. There are many control systems and it is impossible to say which type is best, but generally the control is designed to facilitate the stringing necessary to produce the movements required of the

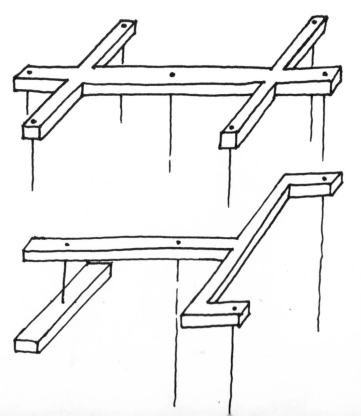

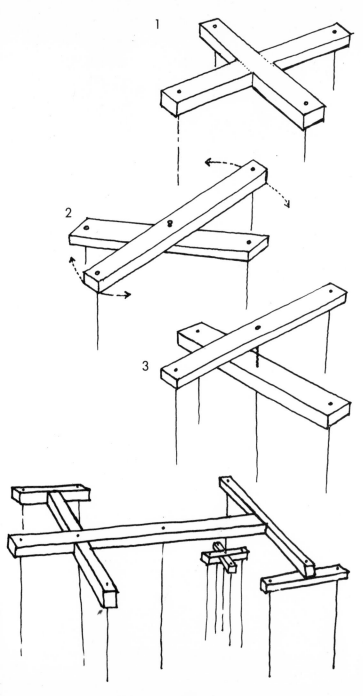

puppet. It is essential that each moving part of the puppet is attached to the control by its separate string. The amount of control exercised over the puppet depends mainly upon the puppeteer's patience, imagination and, above all, willingness to practise. The controls are of three basic types:

1. The rigid cross has a very limited range of movements. It is gripped from above in the palm of the hand and is rocked and turned.

2. The flexible scissors cross has the same range of movement as 1, but gives a slight improvement to the forward movement of the limbs.

3. The third version of the cross control is jointed with a short length of chain or cord, thus permitting each member to move independently. This allows a greater range and more subtle movements.

Also illustrated are examples of controls designed for specific purposes, but you will notice that basically they are cross controls with additional string supports. Only someone with technical skill and imagination should attempt at the beginning the most difficult

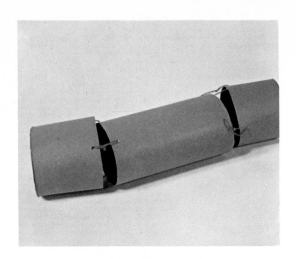

forms of control. The mess of tangled strings resulting when a puppet is dropped is very difficult to sort out. In fact many puppeteers prefer to restring rather than un-tangle. Always aim at the simplest possible form of stringing and control for every puppet you make.

Marionettes from Various Materials

As with abstract puppets, marion-ettes can be constructed from almost anything. The materials employed, if unpainted, can often suggest or reflect the character of the part they play. On the follow-ing pages are illustrated a variety of puppets made from a variety of materials, such as cardboard car-tons and tubes, metal foil, broom-sticks and tin-cans.

A large cardboard tube will serve as a body on to which can be

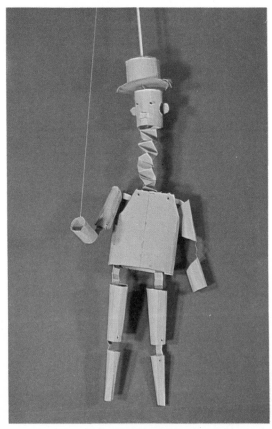

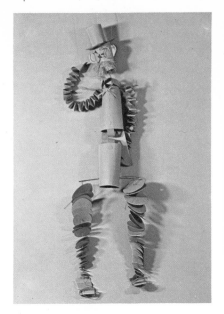

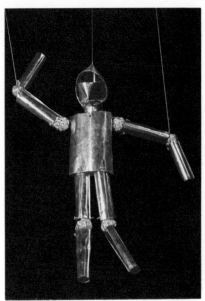

fastened smaller tubes to represent the head and neck, arms and hands and legs and feet, all of which can be flexibly jointed. Simple joints can be made with needle and thread, the number of stitches at each joint determining the degree of flexibility. This is the basic arrangement of parts from which all types of marionette can be constructed. The final appearance of your marionettes will depend upon the diversity of your abilities.

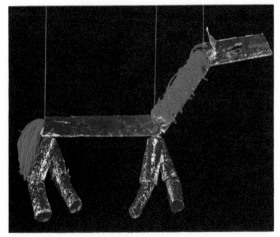

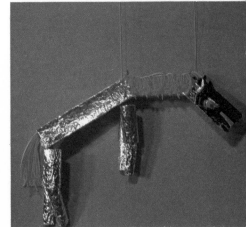

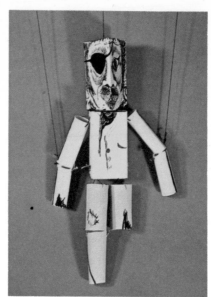

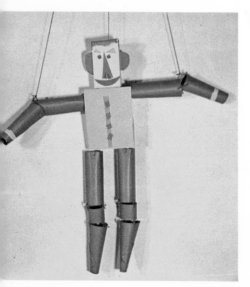

These figures can be painted and/ or decorated with coloured paper, or, if made from coloured cardboard, features can be added in Indian ink.

Cardboard tube figures have, of course, a rather short life: they get soiled and crumpled and lose their attractiveness. But they have set a pattern for figure-building out of separate parts and the only new skills to be learned, when building puppets from a more durable material, are those of jointing. Bodies with formalized limbs can

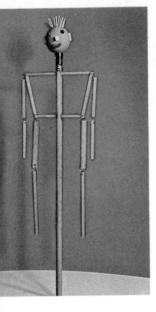

be made from wooden lath or dowel bought in timber yards or hobby shops. Connecting the separate parts can be simple or complex depending on what is required of the joint: a nail hammered into each part and secured with string is simple, but limited. Linked screw eyes provide a simple universal joint for use at the neck, trunk and shoulder. A leather stop-joint can be used at the elbow and knee, etc. The sophisticated marionette will, of course, require its joints to be neater and probably more complex — the puppet on page 36 illustrates this.

Finally a word about hand carving marionettes. It is essential to have good tools. Proper cutting and carving tools can be obtained from hardware and art-supply shops. And if you have access to a

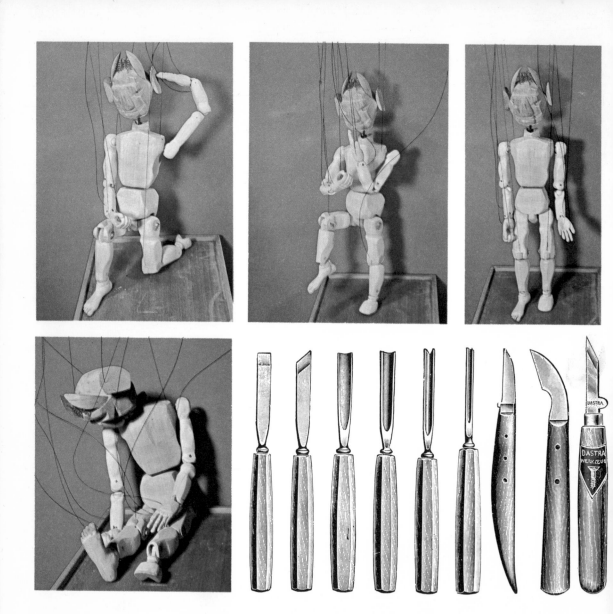

woodwork bench it is advisable from the points of view of facility and safety to use the vice to grip the material with which you are working.

In carpenters' workshops there are all sorts of scraps of wood that, sanded and varnished, can provide the raw material for creating imaginative figures.

36

Should you find that the solid wood marionette is too heavy for prolonged handling, you could make the heads, bodies and limbs lighter by using plastic modelling material, or papier-mâché over polystyrene in the manner described on page 21. The plastic modelling material will give you lightness with reasonable strength, and if the modelling is carefully done screw eyes, cord and leather thongs can easily be worked into the material where they will be gripped as if glued as the puppet hardens.

The marionette is quite a complicated apparatus; it depends upon gravity and needs to be handled intelligently. That is to say, the puppeteer must understand that all the movements he produces are the result of his handling of the strings. If all the strings are released the limbs will hang limply in the inimitable marionette fashion.

In this book we have deliberately shown the simplest forms of control mechanisms. In the illustration above is an extremely intricate example, which permits the movement of head, body and limbs, including hands and feet. Such a control would be designed specifically to fit the hand of the operator normally 'playing' that marionette.

A Small Digression: Puppets and the Trick Film

A word about puppets for those who might enjoy trick cine photography. The inanimate object can be made to appear moving by joining together a series of still photographs, each still being taken after a small alteration in the position of the model. Plasticine figures are ideal for the beginner.

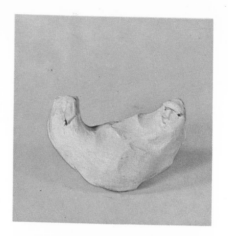

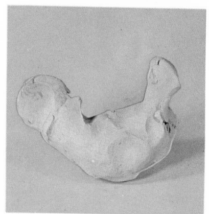

Later, fully modelled figures can be used. For this purpose you will require a model that can remain fixed in each of the positions set. A child's doll is an obvious choice, but how much more satisfying if the model is home-made: for example the stocking puppet, stuffed with rag or sawdust, and with an inner framework of flexible wire permitting the position of the model to be changed step by step.

The World's a Stage

As has been suggested earlier a stage is not absolutely necessary for the production of a puppet play, but such productions are limited in scope without the facilities afforded by the theatre of traditional type. Therefore let us consider two or three simple types of theatre. The shoe-box theatre is perhaps the most simple to make and to operate. Two methods are open to us:

1. If the box is to be held in one hand and the cardboard cut-out puppets operated with the other, the slots by which the puppets are introduced on to the stage will have to be cut right across the floor of the stage from side to side.

2. Greater flexibility of movement can be obtained by inserting the self-supporting figures from the 'wings' through vertical slots in the sides of the box: the puppets being operated by means of rods of wire fastened to the figures at right-angles. With the Shoe-box Theatre resting on a table, both hands are free to operate the puppets.

To cater for larger audiences a bigger, but similar type of theatre can be made from a cardboard carton, into which can be introduced larger puppets and movable scenery. At this stage it becomes feasible to use the other types of puppet, but this will necessitate strengthening and sup-

porting the cardboard carton theatre on a wooden framework. If the floor of the stage is made removable, the one theatre will suffice for most needs. The floor would be removed for the operation of glove and rod puppets from below, and replaced when operating cardboard cut-out puppets from the side, or marionettes from above. Performances will be enhanced if the puppeteers are hidden from the audience's view. This can be achieved quite simply with the addition of a broad cardboard surround suitably painted and decorated.

Scenery can be painted as simply or as detailed as you wish. Sheets of stiff paper, or cardboard will suffice for the short-lived production, but for durability a plastic paint on canvas is advised. In designing your scenery remember the back row of the audience and be bold in proportion and careful in the use of colour: remember that it should not overwhelm the actor. The cardboard backdrop can be made self-standing by folding, but canvas or paper will need a rod at the top and weights at the bottom to enable it to be hung at the back of the stage.

Musical accompaniment presents little difficulty in these days of the portable record player and tape recorder. Sound effects can be produced with very simple apparatus like pot lids, metal foil, peas in a tin or on a tray, etc. But here again the record industry comes to our aid with a wide variety of effects on disc.

Effective lighting is simple to produce but if mains electricity is to be used the *advice of a properly qualified electrician should be obtained.*

Puppetry in School

In the foreword we stated that three aspects of puppetry are educationally valuable: the production, the play itself, and watching and listening. This is, of course, very much a generalization, and it is true to say that it would have no validity at all with education generally or with art and craft particularly if, merely to provide an uncritical fill-in lesson, a half-hearted attempt is made to knock together a puppet of indeterminable character, with an oversimplified script designed only to arouse laughter.

The production of puppets and puppet theatres should always pose some artistic and technical problems.

The play should always have a theme involving language and literature.

Watching and listening should always be an act of involvement with the play.

Finally, we do not just walk into the class and say: 'Today we are going to make puppets!' The idea should originate from some previous occasion and develop according to circumstances — the ages of the children, the requirements of the curriculum and the timetable, and the technical skill of the class.

A desire to make puppets can arise if for some time the children have been modelling and creating character figures that could be given roles to play. When they have completed a number of models the children will often express the wish to make a puppet play. This presents an excellent opportunity of employing puppets to provide a focal point in a lesson. Many subjects can benefit from their use; Language by the writing of a play for production; History by the research involved in tracing the beginnings of puppetry; Geography because puppetry has roots all over the world. In fact, puppetry can provide the basis for an almost total integration of studies.

The simplicity or complexity of the work required of the children will depend largely upon their age, though this does not always follow. Where children have had previous experience of working with paint and clay they will have gained a dexterity and an understanding and feeling for artistic matters that may well be beyond the ability of many adults. Therefore, depending upon the ability of the children and the encouragement they have received, the teacher will determine which project is likely to be the most rewarding.

After a subject for a play has been decided upon there will be considerable competition among the children to model the principal characters. At this point it will pay to discuss the work seriously with all the children, explaining that puppet heads are not the only things of importance to be produced: there are the clothes, the stage and scenery and, eventually, the lighting and sound effects apparatus. The work can then be shared out, each child, or group of children, being assigned a specific task most suited to their abilities.

A promise should be given that all their preparatory work will be utilized in the production of the play. In this way everyone will feel that they have made a really useful contribution. It may be necessary to remind the modellers that their skills, developed when working with clay, papier-mâché, etc., now demand a higher standard of work than that needed in the production of their earlier, primitive Punch and Judy type of figures. It should be explained that, apart from having hands and feet and proper clothes, the features of each head will need to be obviously different. An amusing and simple way of effecting this would be to set a theme of, say, 'The People In Our Town' and to produce caricatures of those best known. Set a theme like 'All Sorts of Strange Beings' and armies of monsters, men from Mars and robots will appear as their imaginations are released to run riot.

The children will be best able to suggest names and characters and voices for the puppets they have made themselves. The groups which have worked together should be encouraged to put on an extempore playlet. This is a particularly fruitful form of activity because such playlets will come directly from the children's imaginations.

The Play

Playing with puppets helps develop a child's empathy for the subject. The ability to feel as though he himself were treading the stage, and mentally acting the puppet's role, develops concentrations and observation. His manipulative skills are also developed as he copes with the problems of translating his wishes to the puppet. It is obvious that, of all the puppets previously described, the marionette with its full range of movements offers the widest opportunities in these respects.

The extempore playlet provides the best opportunities for the child to identify with his puppet partner and to discover new modes of speech, new ways of thinking and a new sense of continuity. He will have to learn to correlate his role with his fellow players. The normal play with its pre-selected roles needs intensive study and interpretation which children may find daunting. For the beginner specially written puppet plays are available that will give confidence and ensure that a more polished performance can be presented to the whole school. Such a performance should be presented and announced as a class effort, for it is definitely not a good thing to pick out a few favoured children, leaving the rest disappointed and resentful.

The most natural combination of subjects are the creative ones of art and language, and it has often been shown that children's vocabularies can be enriched and self-expression made easier through the medium of puppet-play dialogue.

So, in the end, the class has created both the puppet and the play. Rehearsals have shown them who is best fitted for the individual parts and jobs. They have all worked hard and gained many skills, but above all they have learned to work together as a team.

About Watching and Listening
The emphasis so far has been on acquiring practical skills. Let us now consider the value of watching and listening.

We start with the premise that in everything children do they learn something. Therefore, the puppet play should not be a mere vehicle for pleasure and entertainment as its material can be educational in the best sense of the word. Children should be encouraged to watch and listen critically, to judge whether the sense of what the puppet said came across properly. Were the movements appropriate? How could they be improved? Was the language correct? Ought the script to be changed here and there? Are the scenery and props right for the play? Is the play at all boring? Has anything been forgotten?

Children can be a critical audience, but often lack the ability to put their opinions into words. It is, then, a useful experience to let the children play the part of stage director and, with puppet in hand, instruct the other players.

Watching and listening can fulfil a particularly useful function if the teacher through the puppet's mouth gives a 'curtain lecture' or, perhaps, in humorous vein, argues with the puppet on points of grammar, mathematics, etc. The puppet will, of course, always want to answer back!

The puppet play, whatever its standard of perfection, should have its specific place in the classroom. In no other way can so much that is important in life be made immediately and straightforwardly so real — discovering and doing, considering and deciding, judging and improving, learning and enjoying, watching and listening.

In the following pages we go on from what we have already demonstrated and give additional examples of puppet building.

Empty packets and containers offer a host of adventurous possibilities. Puppets made from plastic bottles are specially suited to the rod-puppet theatre for they are light and unbreakable.

Facing page: A rod puppet created from coloured autumn foliage.

Finger puppet made from strong cardboard. Two holes for the first and second finger are cut in the lower part.

Below: Finger puppets 4–6 inches high – 'Auctioneer and Audience' out of 'A Puppet Salad'. Materials used were rubber balls, corks, wool, buttons, and so on. The figures were made first, then little scenes were written suited to the various types.

Simple hand puppets with painted polystyrene heads. Two holes are cut in the sleeveless clothes for thumb and index finger.

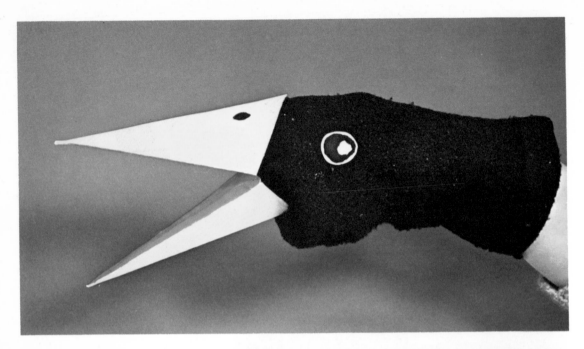

An old stocking or pullover sleeve, cardboard and adhesive are the chief materials for this raven. The beak is opened and closed by the thumb and index finger.

A horse for the hand puppet stage: brush covered with coloured paper.

Facing page: Negro hand puppet. The head is made from a painted polystyrene ball.

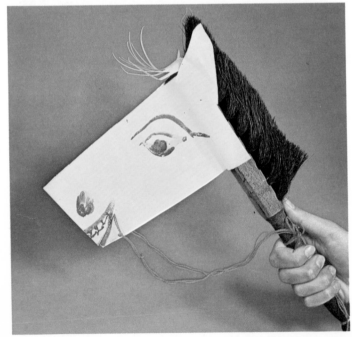

52

Cloth puppet. The head is made
from an old stocking, painted.

Woollen skein puppets can be knitted together from yarn remnants. They are best used as rod puppets (see page 8).

An old piece of tree root painted
with poster colour. One can make
a wide variety of these 'man-
drakes' and a complete root-
theatre can be fashioned. Stuck
on to a stick the rod puppet is
complete.

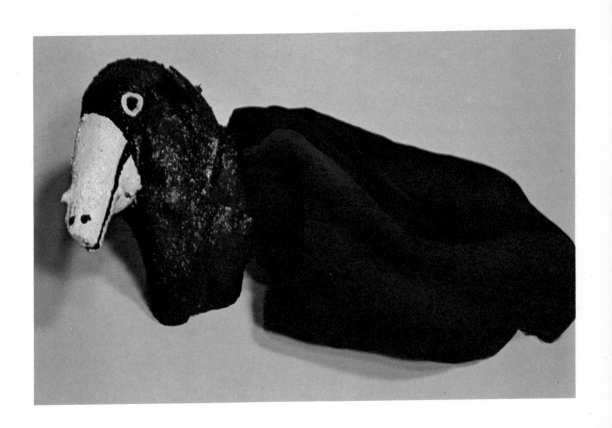

This big raven, a hand puppet, consists mainly of a piece of tree root found in the woods, which was easily carved with a knife and then painted. The hand grasps the lower part of the root inside the cloth covering, and so manipulates it.

A strange paper animal, cut and
folded and strung as a marionette.

58

Bottle figures, 4–18 inches high. From left to right: Karl-Leopold, Professor Brainwave, the Moondog Bibo, and Circus-Director Lookhere from 'Karl-Leopold's Trip to the Moon'. Bottles and decorations from scrap materials. Text devised and written by school children.

Marionette 19 inches high. The Guard from 'The Story of the Clever Woman' by Carl Orff. The materials used, thin sheet metal, industrial waste, cloth, and odds and ends, depended on the character of the figures.

Marionettes 18 inches high. Kaspar and Moneybags, from 'The Magic Fiddle' by Werner Egk. Paper-coated and painted figures staged in the style of the old fair theatre.

Marionettes 12–20 inches high.
'The Short and the Tall Gnome'
from 'Pictures from an Exhibition'.
The production attempted to inter-
pret the music by Mussorgsky
pictorially. The figures are made
from wire, bones, rubber balls,
even a kitchen sieve, and these and
other scrap material were left in
their original form.

Facing page: Rod puppet 36
inches high. 'The Rich Merchant',
made from cardboard, wood and
an electric light bulb.

Glove puppets, 24 inches high. 'Market Women', made from watering cans, sponge-rubber strips, cloth and pearls.

Facing page, above: Rod puppet, 16 inches high, 28 inches wide. A bat made from natural materials, roots, branches, shells, leaves.

Facing page, below: Marionettes 8 and 56 inches high. 'Baba Yaga the Witch and Two Birds'. They were created from roots, branches, bast, willow twigs, fir cones, shells, etc.

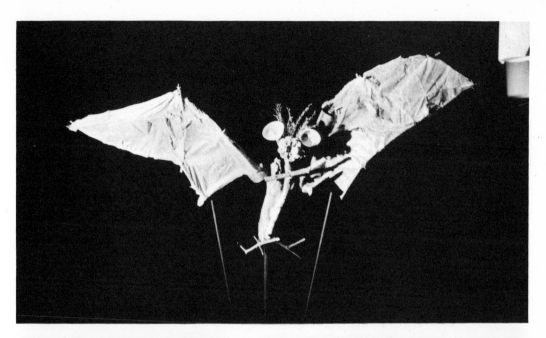